Connections

activities for deductive thinking

Beginning

Written by **Bonnie Lou Risby**
Illustrated by **Jean Thornley**

Reproduction rights granted for single classroom use only.

ROUTLEDGE **Routledge**
Taylor & Francis Group

NEW YORK AND LONDON

First published in 2005 by Prufrock Press Inc.

Published 2021 by Routledge
605 Third Avenue, New York, NY 10017
2 Park Square, Milton Park, Abingdon, Oxon OX14 4RN

Routledge is an imprint of the Taylor & Francis Group, an informa business

ISBN 13: 978-1-5936-3059-1 (pbk)

DOI: 10.4324/9781003233794

Introduction

CONNECTIONS is a thought-provoking puzzle collection that provides challenge and stimulation for the young thinkers in your classroom throughout the entire school year. The purpose of these puzzles is to promote deductive thinking. CONNECTIONS gives students an opportunity to sort throgugh related bits of information by combining, relating, ordering, and eliminating. The result is the logical linking together of ideas that leads to the puzzle's solution.

Each Puzzle in CONNECTIONS has three parts:
1. *The Introduction* — This paragraph sets the background and helps students become familiar with the elements of the puzzle.
2. *The Clues* — The clues relate all of the components and provide a basis for the logical linking together of the pieces of information, thereby allowing students to make deductions that will lead to the solution.
3. *The Grid* — The grid provides a worksheet for sorting, eliminating, and associating the clues. Every square on the grid represents a possible answer. By eliminating possibilities, one is finally left with only one choice per row or column. The one square which has not been eliminated is one correct solution which has been made. When this is done for every row and column, the puzzle solution is complete.

Any marking system for the grid is valid if it is used consistently. Many students prefer to use an X in a square to represent elimination of a choice and an O to represent a correct answer. Using "yes" and "no" works equally well.

In addition to these three parts, students may wish to jot down notes on scratch paper. This may help them in putting the information in rank order or in visualizing the relationships. It should be stressed that there is always more than one way to correctly solve a puzzle; and in sharing the way in which each person used these "tools" to arrive at the solution, students will gain insights into different modes of thinking.

Students will find that it is necessary to look not only at each clue individually, but also to look at the clues in relation to one another in order to derive as much information as possible. For example, if the clues state, "Mary is older than Tom and the girl with the bicycle but younger than Smith," we can deduce a lot of information by the proper arrangement of the clues. If there are only four people in the puzzle, we know that Mary is second in rank of age. If there are two boys and two girls, we also know that Smith is a boy. We can also deduce that Mary is not Smith, Tom is not Smith, Smith is not the one with the bicycle, Mary isn't the one with the bicycle, and Tom isn't the one with the bicycle. In addition, we know that Smith is the oldest.

CONNECTIONS is an ideal way to celebrate the activities and seasons of the school year while incorporating opportunities to strengthen your students' logical, deductive thinking skills. Students will be captivated by the challenge presented by these puzzles, and as they work with these puzzles, they will grow in their ability to sort through information and make important connections.

Table of Contents

Family Occupations

While working on her family tree, Bonnie discovered some members of her family were involved in interesting occupations. Bonnie's cousin, aunt, uncle, mother, father, grandmother, and grandfather are a mayor, dairy farmer, antique dealer, author, conservationist, railroader, and a lumber mill worker.

1. The mayor is married to the man who runs the lumber mill.
2. Ruth runs the dairy farm in Wisconsin.
3. Jerry is Nancy's mother.
4. The author is the niece of the railroader.

5. The lady who sells antiques is the daughter of the mayor and the wife of the railroader.
6. Father is not a conservationist. And he does not run a lumber mill.

Family Tree

While working on her family tree, Bonnie mixed up some of the names. From what she knows, however, she is sure she can put them back in the correct order. Mack, Pearl, Eugene, Jack, Maxine, Nancy, and Judy are Bonnie's cousin, aunt, uncle, mother, father, grandmother, and grandfather.

1. Bonnie knows her mother is Maxine.
2. Jack and Eugene are brothers.
3. Nancy is Judy's daughter.

4. Pearl is the mother of the two sisters.
5. Maxine never met Eugene.

	cousin	aunt	uncle	mother	father	grandfather	grandmother
Mack							
Pearl							
Eugene							
Jack							
Maxine							
Nancy							
Judy							

© Taylor & Francis • *Connections–Beginning*   DOI: 10.4324/9781003233794-2

Family Birthdays

Bonnie, Tonia, Keith, Randy, Jack, Maxine, Marcia, and Kathy have birthdays on November 27, December 4, October 25, August 22, April 3, December 9, July 22, and October 31. Match them.

1. Tonia always went swimming at the river on her birthday.
2. Maxine's birthday is exactly a week before Jack's.
3. The trees are turning beautiful colors on Bonnie's birthday.
4. *Everyone* celebrates on Kathy's birthday.
5. Keith's birthday is exactly one month after Tonia's.
6. Marcia's birthday is celebrated last.

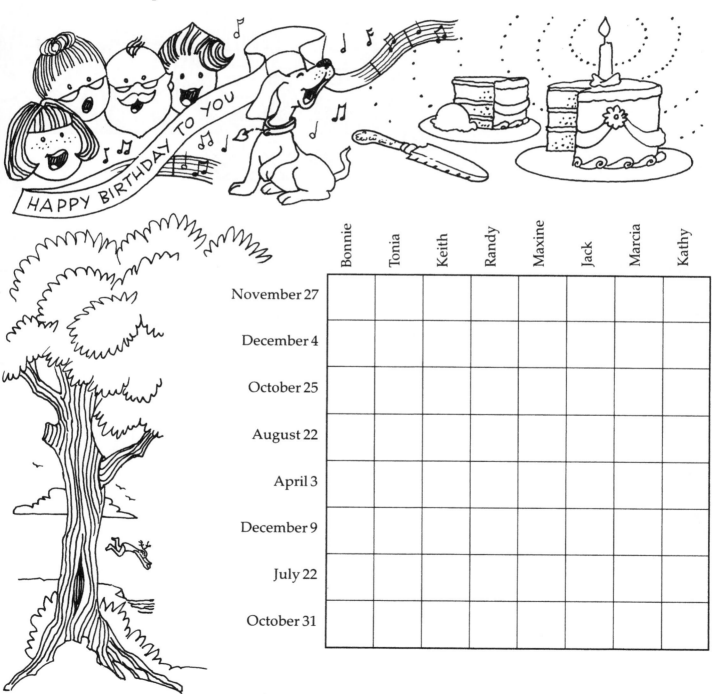

	Bonnie	Tonia	Keith	Randy	Maxine	Jack	Marcia	Kathy
November 27								
December 4								
October 25								
August 22								
April 3								
December 9								
July 22								
October 31								

Thanksgiving

Ann, Mike, Lyn and Bill, whose last names are Juarez, Newton, Myers, and Schuler, each have a favorite Thanksgiving dish—turkey, dressing, cranberry sauce, and pumpkin pie. Sort out the clues and match up everything.

1. Juarez has her favorite dish after the main meal.
2. Mike loves his favorite dish with lots of onion and celery in it.

3. Myers has her favorite dish served in slices (light and dark).
4. Ann hates sweets.
5. Newton is allergic to cranberries.

	Juarez	Newton	Myers	Schuler	turkey	dressing	cranberry sauce	pumpkin pie
Ann								
Mike								
Lyn								
Bill								
turkey								
dressing								
cranberry sauce								
pumpkin pie								

© Taylor & Francis • *Connections–Beginning*　　　　　DOI: 10.4324/9781003233794-4

The Basketball Tournament

Kevin, David, Matthew, and Steve, whose teams are the Eagles, the Wildcats, the Indians, and the Tigers, recently placed 1st, 2nd, 3rd, and 4th in the basketball tournament. Use the clues below to match the players, teams, and how they placed in the tournament.

1. The Wildcats placed ahead of David's team but behind the Tigers.
2. Matthew thinks his team could have placed higher with a little more effort.
3. The Eagles scored ahead of Matthew's team and Matthew's team placed ahead of Steve's.
4. Kevin is not a Tiger.

© Taylor & Francis · *Connections–Beginning*   DOI: 10.4324/9781003233794-5

Christmas Cookies

6

The kids in the neighborhood — Brian, Leila, Matthew, Julie, and Scott — like to get together to decorate Christmas cookies. The cookies are shaped like stars, trees, bells, Santas, and reindeer. The toppings are red sugar, shiny candy balls, raisins, chopped nuts, and and white sugar icing. Each child will decorate only one kind of Christmas cookie. Each cookie is decorated with only one topping. Sift through the clue and see if you can find who decorated which kind of cookie.

1. Leila's cookies are the only ones that must be decorated after they cool.
2. Brian cannot eat his own cookies because he is allergic to nuts.
3. The stars are shiny like the one the three wise men followed.
4. Julie chose a healthy topping that puffed up to look like tree ornaments when they baked.
5. The bells were decorated before baking.
6. The topping for the reindeer gave then the appearance of having a rough brown coat.
7. Matthew spilled his topping and it rolled away in all directions.

© Taylor & Francis · *Connections-Beginning*   DOI: 10.4324/9781003233794-6

Potpourri

Kendra, Laura, Serena, Traci, Cheryl, and Lisa, whose last names are Dotzler, Baz, Andrews, Langley, Staimes, and Hidalgo, are collecting items—rose petals, ginger, honeysuckle blossoms, sage leaves, lemon peels, and cinnamon sticks—to make a potpourri. Sniff your way through the clues to see what each girl contributed.

1. Kendra and Dotzler went to the store to see if they could purchase spices.
2. Serena and Baz and Traci went to a neighbor's garden to collect blossoms and leaves.
3. Andrews has to find lemon peels.
4. The girl looking for cinnamon and Dotzler collected their ingredients before any of the others.
5. Hidalgo has to cut her leaves in half.

6. Cheryl and Staimes had to dry their blossoms.
7. Baz pricked her finger on a thorn while gathering flowers. Laura and Lisa found a bandaid for her.
8. Lisa, the person with ginger, and the person with honeysuckle all three live in the country.
9. Serena and Hidalgo are cousins.

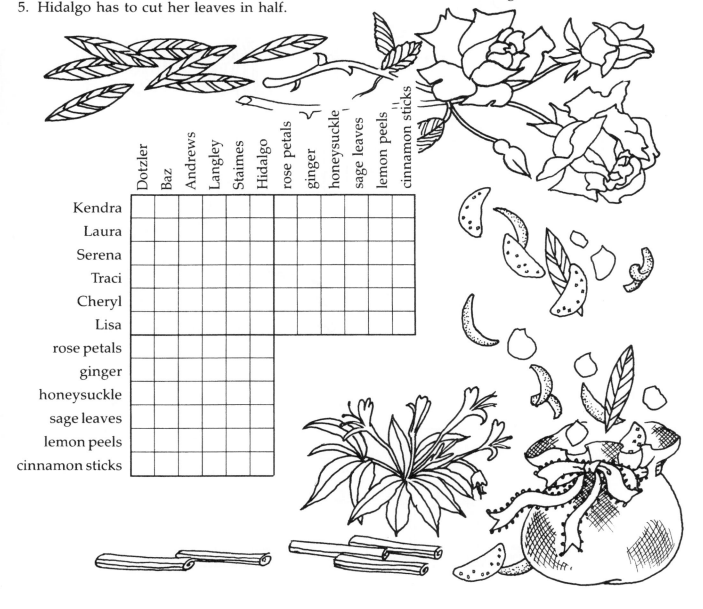

Making Pickles

8

Bob, Bonnie, Connie, and Georgina are making pickles. Each one is in charge of either the cucumbers, the onions, the vinegar, or the sugar. One is peeling, one is slicing, one is measuring, and one is pouring. Their pickling tasks include scrubbing jars, sterilizing lids, stirring the brine, and screwing on the rings. Now see if you can unscramble this pickle. Here are the clues.

1. Connie scrubbed jars, while her brother peeled onions and her sister measured sugar.
2. Georgina poured her ingredient into a pot to boil while she stirred with a wooden spoon.
3. Bob was the strongest so he screwed on the rings.

© Taylor & Francis • *Connections–Beginning*   DOI: 10.4324/9781003233794-8

Fire Drill

During Fire Prevention Week all the classes at Paul Revere School participated in a fire drill. Students from the classes of Mr. Kelly, Mrs. Dominguez, Ms. Stone, and Mrs. O'Reilly, who are in grades 3, 4, 5, and 6, evacuated the building in 30 seconds, 45 seconds, 1 minute 15 seconds, and 1 minute 20 seconds. They left rooms 104, 107, 211, and 212. Fire up your reasoning power as you make your way through the haze of clues and discover the correct solution.

1. Mr. Kelly's class exited quicker than the third grade and the class in room 104, but slower than Ms. Stone's class.
2. Mrs. Dominguez's class and the 5th grade class and the class in room 211 all went out the same exit.

3. Mrs. O'Reilly's class took 5 seconds longer than the sixth grade class.
4. The fourth grade class and Ms. Stone's class have adjoining rooms.

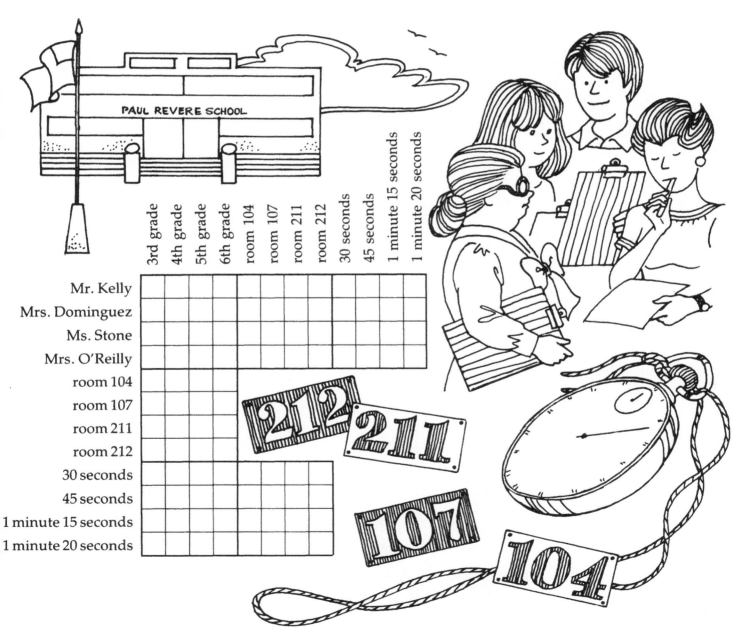

© Taylor & Francis • *Connections–Beginning*   DOI: 10.4324/9781003233794-9

The San Diego Zoo

Mike, Cheryl, Summer, and Crystal Lane recently visited the San Diego Zoo where each found a favorite animal—penguins, elephants, rhinoceros, and leopards. The mother, father, and their two daughters enjoyed a snowcone, animal cookies, ice cream, and coffee while touring the zoo. Parade through the clues and try to snake out the solution to the puzzle.

1. The two sisters liked the penguins and rhinoceros.
2. The person who thought the leopards were the most beautiful enjoyed an ice cream cone.
3. Father blew on his coffee to cool it.
4. Crystal shared her animal cookies with her big sister.
5. Summer asked her father to buy her a cherry snowcone.
6. The youngest person liked the rhino.

DOI: 10.4324/9781003233794-10

When Mary Ann, Paul, Rhonda, Cindy, and Walter, whose last names are Hutton, Levine, Ray, Stuart, and Zanebauer, got together they discussed the different methods they were using to keep fit—jogging, swimming, tennis, golf, and bicycling. Their ages are 16, 18, 21, 22, and 23. Exercise your mind by jogging through these clues to arrive at the proper solution.

1. Hutton is older than her girlfriend who jogs and the boy who plays tennis, but younger than Cindy and the biker.
2. Mary Ann stays in shape with golf.
3. Paul, Levine, Cindy and Zanebauer are all neighbors.

4. Paul is older than Walter but younger than the swimmer.
5. Zanebauer is two years younger than the tennis player.
6. Ray is younger than Stuart.

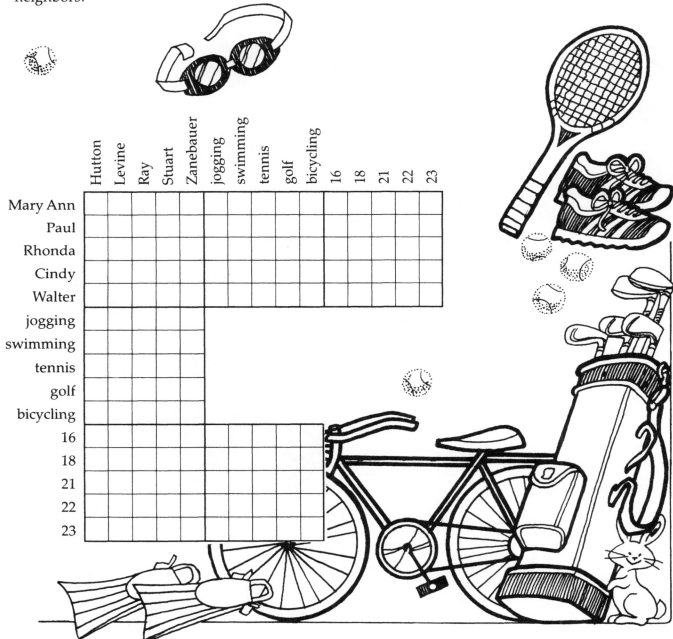

© Taylor & Francis • *Connections–Beginning*

DOI: 10.4324/9781003233794-11

Dog Show

Patti, Keith, Vandria, and Colleen, whose last names are Collins, Vermillion, Hubbard, and Mahoney, entered their dogs—Sundowner, Lord Kimmel, Reflector's Lady, and Homiley Spence— in an all-breed dog show. The dogs, a German shepherd, cocker spaniel, beagle, and collie, received a 1st, 2nd, 3rd, and 4th place award. Now unleash your reasoning on the clues and sniff out the solution.

1. Patti's dog placed ahead of Collins' and the collie, but after Lord Kimmel.
2. Sundowner and the cocker spaniel and Keith's dog were all on leashes.
3. The girl with the German shepherd and the girl with the collie are good friends.
4. Homiley Spence placed ahead of the German shepherd.
5. Hubbard's dog placed after Keith's dog and Reflector's Lady.
6. Colleen's dog placed ahead of the collie.
7. Vermillion's dog placed after the beagle.

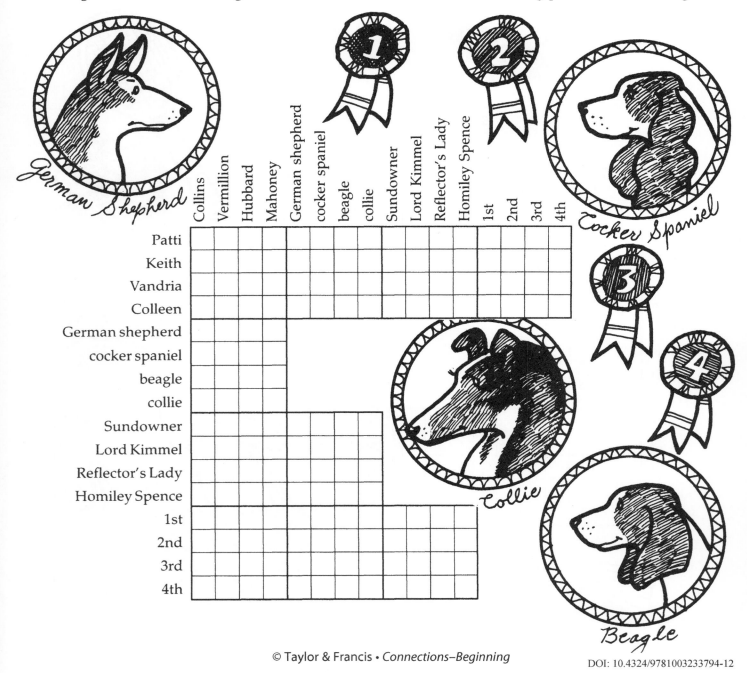

© Taylor & Francis • Connections–Beginning

DOI: 10.4324/9781003233794-12

The Auction

Charlie, Edna, Flora, and Hank, whose last names are Adams, Palladino, Fields, and Johnson, recently went to an auction where they purchased canning jars, an egg incubator, a carnival glass bowl, and a horse collar. The amounts they spent were $3, $10.50, $15, and $18.50. They took their purchases home in a truck, a station wagon, a bicycle, and a farm wagon. Now auction off the clues as you make your bid for a correct match-up.

1. Adams took his purchases home in his wagon pulled by "Old Bly," his horse.
2. Edna spent more than Charlie and the lady who bought canning jars, but less than the person on the bicycle.
3. Fields took the horse collar home.
4. The lady who bought the egg incubator took it home in a truck.
5. Palladino paid $4.50 more than Flora.

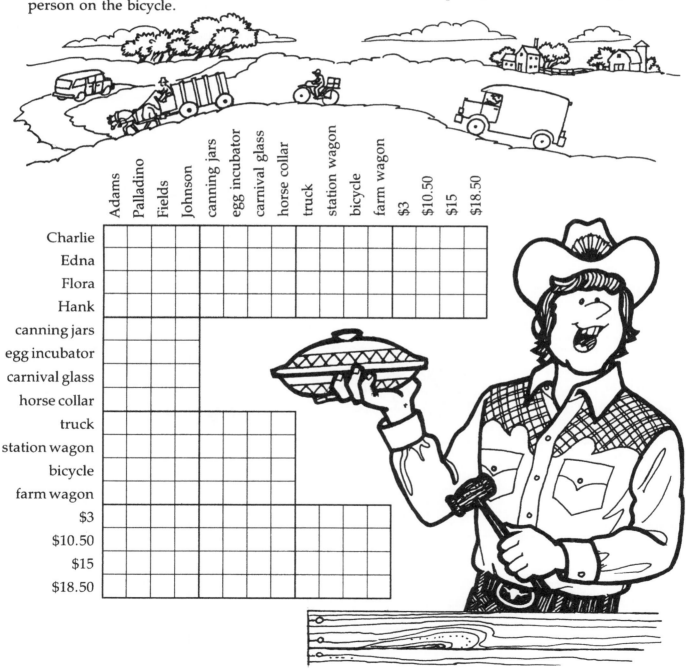

The Float Trip

Four friends decided to take a float trip down the Current River. Bob, Dean, Kyle, and Terry, whose last names are Howerton, Breidecker, Gibson, and Carnahan, each chose to float in a canoe, a john boat, an inner tube, and on a raft. Each one enjoyed a special activity along the way—diving with goggles, swinging from a rope to plunge into the river, skipping rocks, and staging water fights. Each one suffered a minor injury from the outing—mosquito bites, sunburn, a scrape on the chest, and a stubbed toe. See if you can stay afloat by unscrambling the clues and matching up all the facts.

1. Bob, Howerton, and the boy with the john boat got tired of Kyle's water fights.
2. Breidecker scraped his chest on his inner tube valve.
3. Dean and Gibson tied their boats up so one could swing from a rope into the river and the other could skip rocks.
4. The boy in the canoe got a terrible sunburn.
5. Terry asked Breidecker to hold his raft while Terry dived to inspect the river bed with his goggles.
6. Carnahan stubbed his toe while swinging from a rope.

Crocheting

Becky, LaDonne, Jill, and Maria have just learned to crochet. Each girl is making something different—a muffler, a shawl, an afghan, and a vest—and is using a different combination of colors—blue/white, red/white, black/gray, and gold/tan. Also, the girls chose different stitches—single, double, treble, and popcorn—and different patterns—ripple, granny squares, shells, and checkerboard. Now hook the clues together and fashion a correct solution.

1. LaDonne, the girl using blue and white, the girl making a vest, and the girl using the ripple pattern all four learned to crochet from Mrs. Lopes.
2. The afghan is made of single stitch and the muffler is made of treble stitch.
3. The girl using gold and tan is doing a ripple pattern.
4. Becky, Maria, and the girl making the vest are all using size 1 hooks.
5. LaDonne is using a treble stitch and a shell pattern.
6. Becky and the girl making the vest have one color in common.
7. The afghan is done in a ripple pattern.
8. The girl doing the granny squares fastens them together to fashion the vest.
9. The item made of double stitch is in red and white.

   DOI: 10.4324/9781003233794-15

Sorting The Mail

16

Theresa mailed four letters to Donald, Paul, Mark, and Stella, whose last names are Sanborne, Payne, White, and Bradley. They live in Semora, Termo, Fort Hall, and Baileyton in the states of Idaho, North Carolina, California, and Alabama. Their zip codes are 27343, 35019, 83203, and 96132. Sort through the clues and deliver the correct solution.

1. Paul has a higher zip code number than Sanborn and the girl from Alabama, but a lower zip code number than the person in Termo.
2. The zips for Semora and Idaho end with the same digit.
3. Letters to Mark, White, the girl from Baileyton, and the person with zip 96132 all get sorted into different slots at the post office.
4. Stella's zip is higher than Semora's, but lower than Fort Hall's and the one from California.
5. Bradley lives in California.

© Taylor & Francis • *Connections–Beginning*   DOI: 10.4324/9781003233794-16

Keeping In Touch

Four of Mrs. Harper's grandchildren—Scott, Luanne, Randolph, Cindy—whose last names are Gillespie, Davis, Harper, and Lee—went on vacation in July. She received a postcard from each one postmarked July 5, July 19, July 22, and July 30. They were sent from Laurel, Kelso, Heber Spring, and Galivants Ferry in the states of Arkansas, South Carolina, Tennessee, and Washington. Now get in touch with the clues and stamp out the correct answer.

1. Gillespie's card was postmarked before Scott's and the one mailed from Laurel, but after the one from Tennessee.
2. Davis mailed her card from Washington just three days after Randolph mailed his.
3. The postcard from South Carolina was mailed before Luanne's and the one from Heber Spring, but after Cindy's.
4. Harper mailed his card after the one from Galivants Ferry and the one from Lee.

The Hayride

Bob, Dave, Ed, and James, whose dates' names are Lucy, Dianne, Marla, and Sarah, are planning a hayride. Each boy is in charge of getting something for the hayride—wagon, tractor, bonfire, and straw. And each one is in charge of arranging one type of entertainment—horseshoes, volleyball, softball, and a sing-along. The girls are helping with the beverages (coffee, hot chocolate, cider, and soda). Don't get lost in this haystack as you sort everything for the perfect solution.

1. Lucy and Bob's date fixed hot beverages.
2. Ed, the boy getting the tractor, and the boy arranging the sing-along all three arrived after the boy building the bonfire.
3. The girl bringing cider came with the boy bringing the softball equipment and building the bonfire.
4. Marla's date brought his guitar for the sing-along and straw to fill the wagon.
5. James helped his date fix the coffee.
6. Marla and Dianne and Ed's date tried to talk the boys out of having a straw fight.
7. The boy furnishing the tractor also brought the horseshoes.

  DOI: 10.4324/9781003233794-18

This summer Ryan, Cecily, Ed, and Kathy, whose last names are Brogan, Wilde, Macke, and Stimmel, went to the Muny Opera to see *Showboat*. Their seat numbers were 3C, 4C, 5C, and 6C. Each one took something—umbrella, binoculars, cushion, and shawl. Their favorite characters were Captain Andy, Julie, Magnolia, and Gaylord Ravenol. Raise the curtain on the clues and let them light up the solution for you.

1. Brogan and Kathy sat between the boy who liked Captain Andy and the girl who brought a shawl.
2. Wilde and the girl who brought the umbrella borrowed Ed's bincoulars to see particulary interesting scenes.
3. The girl who liked Magnolia and Macke sat in even-numbered seats.
4. Stimmel didn't need her umbrella.
5. Ryan liked Gaylord Ravenol the best.

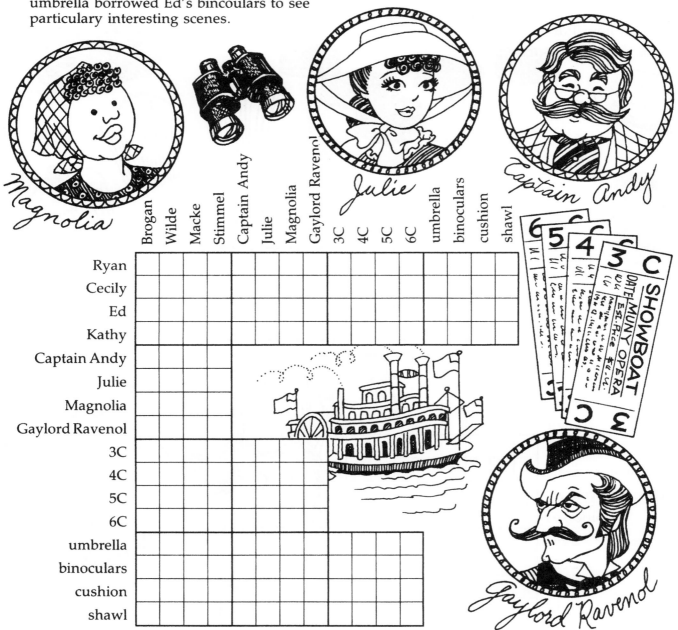

The Bake Sale

Denise, Joy, Natascha, and Shannon, whose last names are Horsley, Garelli, Meyers, and Leigh, are contributing brownies, marshmallow treats, chocolate chip cookies, and cupcakes to a bake sale to raise money for French Club. The girls, who are a freshman, a sophomore, a junior, and a senior, are selling the baked goods for 2/25¢, 2/35¢, 20¢, and 25¢. Make sure you're not half baked as you sift through the clues and whip up the solution.

1. Natascha's goodies are selling for more than the chocolate chip cookies and the goodies brought by the sophomore, but for less than Garelli's.
2. Shannon, Horsley, the junior, and the girl with the brownies all have Mrs. Peterson for 7th hour P.E.
3. The chocolate chip cookies were cheaper than the brownies.
4. The junior made the cupcakes.
5. Joy's brownies are cheaper than Meyers' and the senior's.

Strawberry Picking

Wayne, Becky, Shana, and Jeff, whose last names are Turner, Miller, Crocker, and Wolski, went to pick strawberries for jam, shortcake, frozen berries, and berries with cream. They picked 2, 4, 6, and 14 quarts. They went to the patch at 9 A.M., 10 A.M., 12 P.M., and 1:30 P.M. Don't get in a jam as you pick through the clues to sort out the solution.

1. Becky went to the patch before the person freezing berries and the person picking six quarts, but after Crocker.
2. Shana picked more berries than the person picking berries to go with cream and Jeff, but fewer than the girl making jam.
3. Turner picked two hours earlier than Wolski.
4. The first boy at the patch, the girl making shortcake, and the person picking two quarts brought their own containers.
5. Jeff got to the patch at 1:30 P.M.

Report Cards

Krista, Jennifer, Joshua, and Glenn, whose last names are Miller, Wall, Pulcher, and Hide, got their report cards today. They received 1, 2, 3, and 5 A's. Their best subjects are health, English, math, and reading. Their worst subjects are social studies, spelling, math and science. See if you can score an A in reasoning as you work your way through the following clues.

1. Wall got more A's on her report card than Joshua and the girl who loves English, but fewer than Hide.
2. Joshua's best subject is Krista's worst subject.
3. Jennifer and the girl who loves health and the boy who received one A all ride the same school bus.

4. The person whose worst subject is spelling got more A's than the person whose worst subject is social studies but fewer than the person whose worst subject is science.
5. Miller hates social studies.

© Taylor & Francis · *Connections–Beginning*   DOI: 10.4324/9781003233794-22

Cider Making

Shirley, Rhonda, Doris, and Orville, whose last names are Reed, McDonald, French, and Noblin, are all helping farmer Haynes make apple cider in an old cider press. Farmer Haynes sent each one into various parts of the orchard to gather different varieties of apples—winesap, McIntosh, Jonathan, and red delicious. The helpers, whose ages are 12, 13, 14, and 15, each had a different task in the cider making—filling the hopper, cranking the press, washing the apples, and scrubbing cider bottles. During the cider making each one comments on some different sign of autumn—migrating geese, colored leaves, goldenrod, and ripening pumpkins. Now gather up your wits to see if you can crank out the answer to this puzzle.

1. Shirley is younger than Reed and the boy doing the cranking, but older than the person who gathered the winesaps.
2. McDonald is older than the person filling the hopper and the one who gathered the Jonathans, but younger than the person who spotted the geese.
3. Doris is several years younger than the person scrubbing the bottles and the person who pointed out the goldenrod.
4. Rhonda noticed the chevron of geese honking overhead as she brought in the red delicious apples.
5. French is younger than the person who spied the pumpkins ripening in the field.

DOI: 10.4324/9781003233794-23

The Chinese Restaurant

Four friends—Franci, Rana, Cheryl, and Jessie—whose last names are Lebow, Dixon, Freeman, and Raitt—decided to visit the Golden Dragon Chinese restaurant. Egg foo yung, chicken chow mein, won ton soup and shrimp kew are the dishes they chose for lunch. Each spent a different amount—$1.25, $3.95, $4.05, and $4.30, Two girls used forks to eat while the others chose chopsticks and a spoon. After the meal each girl received a fortune cookie promising various events—become wealthy, become a success, become wise, and become humble. Use your most clever Chinese detective reasoning to unscramble this mystery and match up everything.

1. Dixon's lunch was more expensive than Franci's and the girl's who ordered the egg foo yung.
2. Cheryl is allergic to seafood.
3. Jessie's lunch cost less than the girl's who used chopsticks and the girl's whose fortune cookie promised wealth.
4. Shrimp kew cost nearly four times what Franci paid for the soup.

5. Franci, Raitt, and the girl's whose fortune cooky said she was humble all drank hot tea.
6. Raitt's lunch was $.25 less than the girl whose cooky predicted she would become wealthy.
7. Freeman used a soup spoon.
8. The girl with chopsticks ate chow mein.
9. Cheryl's fortune predicted she would become wise.

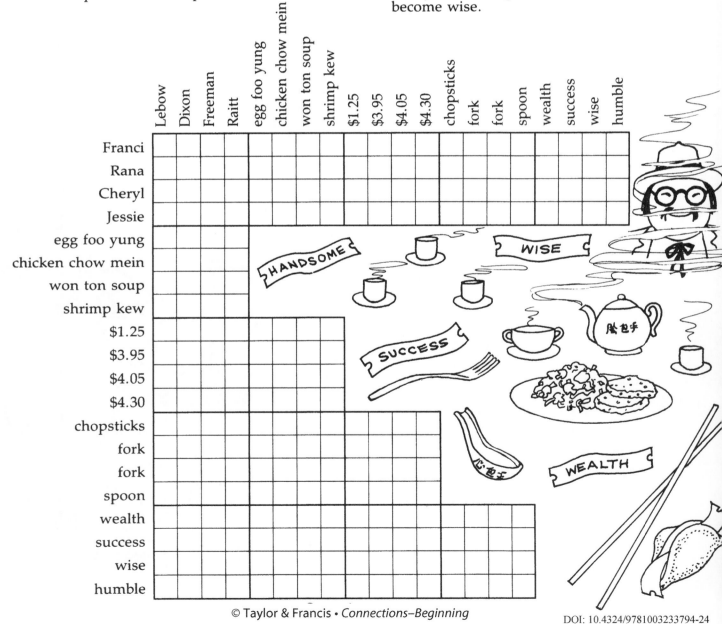

DOI: 10.4324/9781003233794-24

Answers

1. Family Occupations
Grandfather – lumber mill
Father – railroader
Uncle – conservationist
Cousin – author
Grandmother – mayor
Mother – antique dealer
Aunt – dairy farmer

2. Family Tree
Mack - grandfather
Pearl - grandmother
Eugene - uncle
Jack - father
Maxine - mother
Nancy - cousin
Judy - aunt

3. Family Birthdays
Bonnie – October 25
Tonia – July 22
Keith – August 22
Randy – April 3
Marcia – December 9
Jack – December 4
Maxine – November 27
Kathy – October 31

4. Thanksgiving
Ann Myers – turkey
Mike Newton – dressing
Lyn Juarez – pumpkin pie
Bill Schuler – cranberry sauce

5. The Basketball Tournament
1st – Eagles – Kevin
2nd – Tigers – Matthew
3rd – Wildcats – Steve
4th – Indians – David

6. Christmas Cookies
Brian – reindeer, nuts
Leila – Santas, icing
Matthew – stars, shiny balls
Julie – trees, raisins
Scott – bells, red sugar

7. Potpourri
Kendra Langley – cinnamon sticks
Laura Dotzler – ginger
Serena Staimes – honeysuckle
Traci Hidalgo – sage leaves
Cheryl Baz – rose petals
Lisa Andrews – lemon peels

8. Making Pickles
Bob – onions, peeling, screwing on lids
Bonnie – sugar, measuring, sterilizing lids
Connie – cucumbers, slicing, scrubbing jars
Georgina – vinegar, pouring, stirring

9. Fire Drill
Mr. Kelly – 4th, room 211, 45 seconds
Mrs. Dominguez – 6th, room 104, 1 minute
    15 seconds
Ms. Stone – 5th, room 212, 30 seconds
Mrs. O'Reilly – 3rd, room 107, 1 minute
    20 seconds

10. The San Diego Zoo
Mike – father, elephants, coffee
Cheryl – mother, leopards, ice cream
Summer – daughter, penguins, snowcone
Crystal – daughter, rhinoceros, animal cookies

11. Keeping Fit
Mary Ann Hutton – golf, 21
Paul Ray – bicycling, 22
Rhonda Zanebauer – jogging, 16
Cindy Stuart – swimming, 23
Walter Levine – tennis, 18

12. Dog Show
Patti Vermillion – cocker spaniel, Homiley Spence,
    2nd
Keith Mahoney – beagle, Lord Kimmel, 1st
Vandria Hubbard – collie, Sundowner, 4th
Colleen Collins – German shepherd, Reflector's
    Lady, 3rd

13. The Auction
Charlie Adams – carnival glass bowl, farm wagon,
    $3
Edna Palladino – egg incubator, truck, $15
Flora Johnson – canning jars, station wagon,
    $10.50
Hank Fields – horse collar, bicycle, $18.50

14. The Float Trip
Bob Gibson – canoe, skip rocks, sunburn
Dean Carnahan – john boat, swinging on rope,
    stubbed toe
Kyle Breidecker – inner tube, water fight, scraped
    chest
Terry Howerton – raft, goggles, mosquito bites

15. Crocheting
Becky – blue/white, popcorn stitch, shawl,
    checkerboard
LaDonne – black/gray, treble stitch, muffler, shell
Jill – red/white, double stitch, vest, granny squares
Maria – gold/tan, single stitch, afghan, ripple

16. Sorting the Mail
Donald Bradley – Termo, California, 96132
Paul White – Fort Hall, Idaho, 83203
Mark Sanborn – Semora, North Carolina, 27343
Stella Payne – Baileyton, Alabama, 35019

17. Keeping In Touch
Scott Harper – Heber Spring, Arkansas, July 30
Luanne Davis – Laurel, Washington, July 22
Randolph Gillespie – Galivants Ferry, South
     Carolina, July 19
Cindy Lee – Kelso, Tennessee, July 5

18. The Hayride
Bob – Marla, straw, sing-along, hot chocolate
Dave – Dianne, bonfire, softball, cider
Ed – Sarah, wagon, volleyball, soda
James – Lucy, tractor, horseshoes, coffee

19. Showboat
Ryan Brogan – Gaylord Ravenol, 5C, cushion
Cecily Wilde – Julie, 3C, shawl
Ed Macke – Captain Andy, 6C, binoculars
Kathy Stimmel – Magnolia, 4C, umbrella

20. The Bake Sale
Denise Horsley – freshman, chocolate chip
     cookies, 2/25¢
Joy Leigh – sophomore, brownies, 2/35¢
Natascha Meyers – junior, cupcakes, 20¢
Shannon Garelli – senior, marshmallow treats, 25¢

21. Strawberry Picking
Wayne Crocker – berries/cream, 4 quarts, 9 A.M.
Becky Turner – jam, 14 quarts, 10 A.M.
Shana Wolski – shortcake, 6 quarts, 12 P.M.
Jeff Miller – frozen berries, 2 quarts, 1:30 P.M.

22. Report Cards
Krista Wall – 3 A's, health, math
Jennifer Pulcher – 2 A's, English, spelling
Joshua Miller – 1 A, math, social studies
Glenn Hide – 5 A's, reading science

23. Cider Making
Doris French – 12, filling hopper, winesap, leaves
Shirley Noblin – 13, washing apples, Jonathan,
     pumpkins
Orville McDonald – 14, cranking press, McIntosh,
     goldenrod
Rhonda Reed – 15, scrubbing bottles, red
     delicious, geese

24. The Chinese Restaurant
Franci Freeman – won ton soup, $1.25, spoon,
     success
Rana Dixon – shrimp kew, $4.30, fork, wealth
Cheryl Raitt – chicken chow mein, $4.05,
     chopsticks, wise
Jessie Lebow – egg foo yung, $3.95, fork, humble

For Product Safety Concerns and Information please contact our EU representative GPSR@taylorandfrancis.com Taylor & Francis Verlag GmbH, Kaufingerstraße 24, 80331 München, Germany

T - #0081 - 090625 - C0 - 279/216/2 - PB - 9781593630591 - Gloss Lamination